Snow Dreams

David Jaffin

Snow Dreams

As Rosemarie (3) 73

A Different (2) 74

Flag-Wavers (4) 75

Is taste a (7) 76

Perspective (4) 78

He maintain (4) 79

Talk-show (4) 81

A post Trump (3) 82

Though (4) 83

Cloud-worship (4) 84

Unreliable (2) 85

Good grade (2) 86

Half-deaf (2) 87

Transition (4) 88

The Yellow (5) 89

A generat (7) 90

Light-blue (3) 92

Appropriate- (4) 93

Left-behind (4) 94

Landscaping (3) 95

Outused- (3) 96

Advertising (2) 97

After read (4) 98

Drunken (5) 99

I could perhap (3) 101

Self-recept 102

Why do only (11) 102

"Be thankful (6) 106

As they say (3) 108

Being both 109

Poetry (4) 109

Why (4) 111

"No sooner (2) 112

Side-street (10) 113

Friendship (12) 116

It's most (7) 120

Ode to the (4) 122

Spotty (4) 123

Churchless (2) 124

To believe (4) 125

Why do I (3) 126

Together (4) 127

They've e (3) 128

A là Swift (4) 129

The remain 130

Looking
through (3) 130

That once ex (3) 131

Qualitie (2) 132

Written from (4) 133

Northern (2) 134

Du Fu and (7) 134

Answering (3) 137

No I'm not (9) 138

Some even (4) 141

Whether (2) 142

A freshly (2) 142

Is snow then (2) 143

Even I (2) 144

Believe it (2) 144

Yes some Chin (4) ... 145

It may create (4) 147

Perhaps (2) 148

One sense (2) 148

When one (3) 149

This self- (2) 150

Piled-high (3) 151

As "we hurt (2) 152

This land' (5) 152

Awakening (2) 154

America (6) 155

The impend (3) 157

At the road (3) 158

It's a real (2) 159

Battlefield (4) 160

Inky only (7) 161

This Bavar (2) 163

A most necess (3) 164

The long- (3) 165

Superlatives (5) 166

If white' (3) 168

Every (2) 169

Sounds like (7) 169

Thinking 172

If you allow 172

Why do we (4) 173

This snow' (3) 174

Light-blue (3) 175

Poem (2) 176

The early (3) 177

The poet (3) 178

Book shelve (3) 179

Doctor' (3) 180

Streetlight (3) 181

When he re (3) 182

Trying to (3) 183

This partial (3) 184

I've often (3) 185

Freedom to be
free (6) 186

A world of (3) 188

Does over- (7) 189

Spanish-Span (4) 191

Complement (8) 192

Our prayer- (3) 194

Yet Yet Yet (5) 195

Tiny but (3) 197

These once (2) 198

It must re (4) 199

Looking away (5) 200

Little bird (3) 201

Memories of (4) 202

7

Picture (3)...............203
We may (3) 204
Time and (3) 205
For a young.............206
Otherwise (3)..........206
Unlined (2) 207
Good poetry (2) 208
Some person' (4) 209
Those momen (5)....210
That snow- (3) 211
My window' (2) 212
Developmental
Phases (3)................213
Girls became (2) 214
Butter finger (4) 215
For G. H. (3)...........216
Slow-poke (4) 217
This unsea (4) 218
These tiny...............219
This after 219
As G. H. 220
Although (3) 221
Those most (4)........222
Is there an (2) 223
Mixed-loyalitie
(12)..........................224
If I said (4)..............228
These ever- (7)........229

For the (3)...............231
For G. H.' 232
Strangely (3)............233
For G. H..................234
Here in Cor (4) 235
666 the bibli (3).......236
Those Jew- (5) 237
The highest (4)........239
Symbolical (2) 240
Baby-faced (3).........241
Only 83 (4)..............242
Safe in the (5)..........243
Even in voice (5) 245
G. H........................246
To the memory (4) ..247
Lip-service (5)..........248
Both of my (4) 249
I continue (4) 251
Light-warmth
revival (3)................252
Poet-in-Re (4) 253
That unusual (3)......254
Autobiograph (3).....255
Is this (4)..................256
It could only (5) 257
If my physio (3) 259
Matthew (6)............260
This day (4)..............262

The unsaid- (3) 263
Prodigal (4) 264
Not only (5) 265
Alchemist
(Spitzweg) (3) 267
Perhaps we've (4) 268
Lullaby (4) 269
Was that hea (2) 270
Falling' (7) 271
Translation (5) 273
No one (4) 275
Tiredness (4) 276
It's now (6) 277
Disgrace (3) 279
Letter-of-the (2) 280
Doomsday (4) 280
February 1 (4) 282
One Pleasure (5) 283
This (now) (3) 285
Yes it's (4) 286
One could (2) 287
How Chinese (4) 288
Why Haydn of
all (5) 289
Yes a relat (3) 291
A Resumée (5) 292
Off-timed (4) 293
At Face Value (3) 295

Too late to (4) 296
Imprisoned (4) 297
Du and Sie (3) 298
Spelling-it- (4) 299
For Solvey (8) 300
Fences (4) 302
The taste (6) 303
Doris and (6) 305
They went so (2) 307
These repeti (2) 308
Her softly 308
How easily (3) 309
Was it a com (2) 310
They'd all be (2) 311
Early Februa (3) 312
"It takes (3) 313
Owl-eyed 314
"Les Jeux sont (4) 315
A genuine (3) 316
Mapped-out (5) 317
P. S. (3) 319
I guess The (3) 320
Unoccupied (3) 321

*Poetry books
by David Jaffin* *322*

9

With continuing thanks for
Marina Moisel
preparing
this manuscript

and to Hanni Bäumler
for her well-placed
photograph

If I had to classify my poetry, it could best be done through the classical known "saying the most by using the least". The aim is thereby set: transparency, clarity, word-purity. Every word must carry its weight in the line and the ultimate aim is a unity of sound, sense, image and idea. Poetry, more than any other art, should seek for a unity of the senses, as the French Symbolists, the first poetic modernists, realized through the interchangeability of the senses: "I could hear the colors of her dress." One doesn't hear colors, but nevertheless there is a sensual truth in such an expression.

Essential is "saying the most by using the least". Compression is of the essence. And here are some of my most personal means of doing so turning verbs into nouns and the reverse, even within a double-context "Why do the leaves her so ungenerously behind". Breaking words into two or even three parts to enable both compression and the continuing flow of meaning. Those words must be placed back together again, thereby revealing their inner structure-atomising.

One of my critics rightly said: "Jaffin's poetry is everywhere from one seemingly unrelated poem to the next." Why? Firstly because of my education and interests trained at New York University as a cultural and intellectual historian. My doctoral dissertation on historiography emphasizes the necessary historical continuity. Today we often judge the past with the mind and mood of the present, totally contrary to their own historical context. I don't deny the past-romanticism and classical but integrate them within a singular modern context of word-usage and sensibility. Musically that would place me within the "classical-romantic tradition" of Haydn, Mozart, Mendelssohn, Brahms and Nielsen but at the very modern end of that tradition.

My life historically is certainly exceptional. My father was a prominent New York Jewish lawyer. The law never interested me, but history always did. A career as a cultural-intellectual historian was mine-for-the-asking, but I rejected historical relativism. That led me to a marriage with a devout German lady – so I took to a calling of Jesus-the-Jew in post-Auschwitz Germany. For ca. two decades I wrote and lectured all over Germany on Jesus the Jew. Thereby my knowledge and understanding of both interlocked religions became an essential part of my being. History, faith and religion two sides of me but also art, classical music and literature were of essential meaning – so many poems on poetry, classical music and painting.

Then Rosemarie and I have been very happily married for 60 years now. Impossible that a German and Jew could be so happily married so shortly after the war? I've written love poems for her, hundreds and hundreds over those 60 years, not only the love poems, as most are, of the first and often unfulfilling passion, but "love and marriage go together like a horse and carriage". Perhaps too prosaic for many poets?

When did I become a poet? My sister Lois wrote reasonably good poetry as an adolescent. I, only interested in sports until my Bar Mitzvah, a tournament tennis and table-tennis player, coached baseball and basketball teams, also soccer.

My sister asked whether I'd ever read Dostoyevsky. I'd only read John R. Tunis sports books and the sports section of the *New York Times* so I answered "in which sports was he active?" She said, rather condescendingly, "If you haven't read Dostoyevsky, you haven't lived." So I went to the library for the very first time and asked for a book by this Dostoyevsky. I received *Poor People*, his first book, that made him world famous. My mother shocked to see me reading and most especially a book about poor people said, "David, don't read that it will make you sad, unhappy – we, living in Scarsdale, weren't after all, poor people. From there it went quickly to my Tolstoy, Hardy and so on. In music it started with the hit parade, then *Lost in the Stars*, then the popular classics and with 15 or 16 my Haydn, Mozart, Schütz, Victoria... And then at Ann Arbor and NYU to my artists, most especially Giovanni Bellini, Van der Weyden, Georges de la Tour, Corot and Gauguin...

But it was Wallace Stevens' reading in the early 50s in the YMHA that set me off – he didn't read very well, but his 13 Ways of Looking at a Blackbird, Idea of Order at Key West, Two Letters (in *Poems Posthumous*), Peter Quince at the Clavier, The Snowman... and the excellent obituary in *Time* magazine plus the letter he answered some of my poems with compliments but "you must be your own hardest critic". That pre-determined my extremely self-critical way with a poem. Please don't believe that prolific means sloppy, for I'm extremely meticulous with each and every poem.

My poems were published in the order written and I'm way ahead of any counting... The poem is a dialogical process as everything in life. The words come to me not from me, and if they strike or possibly join-a-union then I become desparate, read long-winded poets like Paz to set me off – he's very good at odd times. Those poems need my critical mood-mind as much as I need their very specially chosen words – not the "magic words" of the romantics, but the cleansed words of Jaffin – Racine used only 500 words. My words too are a specially limited society, often used, but in newly-felt contexts.

O something very special: I have a terrible poetic memory. If I had a good one as presumably most poets, I'd write say one poem about a butterfly, and every time I see/saw a butterfly it would be that one, that poem. But I forget my poems, so each butterfly, lizard, squirrel... is other-placed, other-mooded, other-worded, other-Jaffined. That's the main reason why I am most certainly the most prolific of all poets.

Shakespeare is the greatest of us: his sonnets live most from the fluency and density of his language. I advise all future poets to keep away from his influence and the poetic greatness of The Bible.

Yours truly
David Jaffin

P. S.: As a preacher the truth (Christ) should become straight-lined, timelessly so, but as a poet it's quite different. What interests me most are those contradictions which live deeply within all of us, not only in theory, but daily in the practice. And then the romantics have led me to those off-sided thoroughly poetic truths that mysteriously not knowing where that darkened path will lead us.

Poetry Book 112

January 15 – February 3, 2021

For Warren

Icicles

hanging sword–
length the

blood region
s of Beowulf

s primevil
world.

Though in *(4)*

a) his late 50s

he woke-

up one other
wise morning

b) to discover

his own mirr

ored feature
s had taken-

on new and

c) unfamiliar

appearance
s This heavy

mid-January
snow had

d) remade Illmen

see's landscap

ing in its
own cleansed

indelible-i
mage.

A lost Forget *(2)*

a) fulness This

snowed-down

wintered
tree direct

ly opposite

b) our Illmen

see's living-
room seems

burdened with
the unduly

weight of a
lost-forget

fulness.

Reicha' *(5)*

a) s wind music

most always
s appeals to
vacation

b) ed less pro

found sensi
bilitie

s This Beet
hoven contem

c) porary-friend

endears one
to its light

er transpar
ent-impuls

d) ive-express

iveness and
his love of

the personal
intimate fla

e) vour of each

of the wind
instrument'

s pre-Nielsen
-like.

Why am I es (3)

a) *pecially attract*

ed to double-

fugues Zelenka'
s and Mozart'

b) *s Is it the*

contrary dir
ection of

their unify

ing-presence
poetically

c) *quite simil*

ar to my es
pecial use of

(implied) ambig
uities.

It snowed

through the
night releas

ing the depth
of darkly i

magined sha
dowings as

we awoke to
its dreamed

purifying-
presence.

Such a deep (2)

a) ly self-inhab

iting snow

here in Illmen
see that its

very presence

b) weighted-me-

down to the
recurring

need for a
self-securing

time-hold.

They're the (3)

    a) rare exception

    s today These

    readers as my
    sister Doris

    b) in their care

    fully-selected-

    books that
    their oft un

    answered mess

    c) age left her

    at times to
    a soundless

    vacancy-from-
    self.

Perhaps (6)

a) Street-dog'

s owners as
Andreas and

Annette's

b) 4 may real

ise a very
significant

advantage
for their a

c) depted own

ers a perhap

s almost un
limited thank

fulness for

d) saving them

from a perpet
ual fear of

an anonymous
if pre-deter

e) mining death

The numerous

owners here
of children

taken out of

f) distant slum

s may become
in time a spec

ially-recurr
ing thankful

ness.

One and a *(5)*

a) half Barbara'

s little half-

black attract
ive daughter

b) continues to

receive more

than a single
child's usual

especially en

c) dowed love

while receiv
ing what a

dedicated
father-husband

d) would have

called his own

if he'd become
the biblical

e) Jacob's lov

ing stay-at–

home dedicated
husband and

father.

Those prior (3)

a) 2 days of

intensing

snow has
left the small

lake-down

b) town of Ill

mensee such
a dominating

snow-encompass
ing newly-veri

fied-self that

c) it continue

s to remain
habitually

motionless
ly self-satis

fied.

"It was snow (4)

> *a) ing and it*
>
> was going to
>
> snow" Wallace
> Stevens' histor

> *b) ic January*
>
> Connecticut
>
> landscape
> remains so
>
> self-suffic

> *c) iently true*
>
> that it speak
>
> s the same
> language
>
> here in the

> *d) so histor*
>
> ically dis
> tant Illmen
>
> see even de
> cades–later.

Under (7)

a) standing's

more encompass

ing than analy
sing the sym

b) bolic meaning

s of say med

ieval relig
ious art

That's actual

c) ly ever-stand

ing it with
a secular

sense of im
plicit super

d) iority Under

standing's

actually just
that a compass

ionate feel

e) ing for a

transmitting
faith If you'

re agnostic
better to

f) deal with a

really under

standing art
of secular–

modernism

g) As Rosemarie

likes so say
"the tone

makes the
music".

However (4)

a) much we may

prefer it o

therwise Life'
s not one of

b) those even-

steven thing

s It's full
of its own

jolts and star–

c) gazing surprise

s Don't try
to be prepar

ed because

d) it's always

on your-beat
continual

ly preparing
you for.

It was like (4)

   a) entering a pre-

   historic cave

   untouched
   beyond time'

   b)s penetrat

   ing darkness

   es wombed for
   its own self–

   inhabiting
   water–expect

   c) ant stillness

   Early morn

   ing distant
   car lights

   as if called
   to awaken

   d) this snow-

   bound land

   to its pre–
   assuming quiet

   udes.

St. Corona (4)

a) *even spoiled*

the big cele

brations
for the mighty

Beethoven's
250th bring

b) *ing-him-down*

to an other

wise perspect
ive **Du Fu**

little
known during

his own life

c) *time died in*

near poverty
though awaken

ed a few cen
turies later

from his un
honored grave

d) to a lasting

poetic-signi

ficance Taste
changes art

ists don't (at
least in that

respect).

Dangling *(3)*

a) pre-position

s as Shakes

peare well-
realised re

b) main hanging

with a no

longer possi
ble attainable

conclusive

c) ness as a

fisherman'
s line spac

iously time-
expectant.

January 18 *(4)*

a) How such a

little vaccine
ation needle

could make
such a big

b) difference

(more than

skin-deep)
for your fu

ture life-ex

c) pectancie

s How such
an interchange

able 1 or 2

d) letters could/

should avail
such a time-

exposing diff
erence.

This snow (2)

> a) *seems here-to-*
>
> stay so that
>
> it may have
> lost its poet
>
> ic–metaphysi
> cal presence

> b) *Yes even its*
>
> weight a bit
>
> lessened
> through its
>
> habitually
> sensed–therea
>
> bouts.

Bird of the (5)

> a) *Year It's best*
>
> if you're quali
>
> fied (flying
> tests possible

b) here) to vote

from 10 pre-

chosen birds of
the year that

you may be

c) come aware of

their intri
cate color

ings the
poetry of their

d) flight-habit

s (whether

wintering
or not) Is

it really a

e) genuine beauty-

contest or
one of sheer

individual–
survival.

"Pull your (3)

    a) self together"

    as if we'd

    become no
    longer whole

    b) as if the

    mind and the

    body had dis
    oriented

    and become

    c) as puppets

    in need of
    others to

    pull the nec
    essary-string

    s.

No (3)

a) first press

the button

No that re
petitive ans

wer flashed–

b) out even be

fore the mind
could function

the lips could
answer No as

if her life
had become

c) nothing more

than a con

tinual self–
denying pro

cess.

I don't like *(3)*

> *a) lines especial*

ly because
of my Jaffin–

impatience
to get thing

> *b) s done and*

over with but

such lines
still remote

ly remind me
of the one'

> *c) s where there'*

s a 97% sure

ty of a no–
return-tick

et.

The far *(5)*

> *a) less-than-pre*

cocius–poet

continued
to believe

b) in the chim

ney–present

descending–
Santa Claus

though remain

c) ed uncertain

whether those
reindeer could

fit through
his most remem

bered quote

d) from those

early years
"When I grow

up to be a
girl as my

sisters I

e) want to join

them in the
summer at

camp Red–
Wing."

Retrieving *(3)*

a) Back to snow-

bound Illmen

see retriev
ing as the

b) family dog'

s mouthpiece

my own poet
ic one for a

lasting use
of "those

c) real winter

s we used

to have" snow-
bound in per

petual-remem
brance

s.

Shouldn't *(3)*

a) form become a

most natural

endeavor of
the linguist

b) ic unifying-

process of

the poem's
oncoming rai

son d'être

c) Why need of

pre-given
forms for their

own sake's
acceptance.

After Gauguin (3)

a) On the move

again that

transient
feeling of

b) "where do we

come from"

momentarily
neither here

nor there's

c) "What are

we" uncertain
ly maintain

ing "where
are we go

ing".

Purgatoried *(3)*

a) If that vaccin

ation takes
6 to 8 week

s for its
full 95% cover

b) age (which I'

ve come to

disbelieve)
what if we

died in the
midst of that

c) lengthening-

process purga

toried of our
long-expect

ant hope
s.

Suffocating (2)

a) These winter-

bared tree

s impression
a sense of

suffocating
under the

b) snow-mounds

of this

severe mid–
January ex

pressive
ness.

Merkel (2)

a) an inbred

scientist

in her own
right should

know better
than to fully

b) trust the de

viant and

often devious
methods of

the so-call
ed "expert

s".

Trumpism *(2)*

a) Some person

s even quite

bright one
s hear what

they want-to-
hear even

b) though the

evidence

speaks an
otherwise

language-
of-its-own.

The sky's *(3)*

> *a) heavenly sour*
>
> ced winter
>
> blue and the
> late January

> *b) sun brighten*
>
> ing the long
>
> since fallen
> snow's earth-
>
> bottomed re
> ceptively a

> *c) waiting a*
>
> timeless
>
> ly fully-a
> dapting ans
>
> wering-call.

Thaw (2)

a) The winter'

s ground–

clutching
snow loosen

ing its cer

b) taining grasp

releasing
streams of

heart-felt
sovereign-ex

pectation
s.

Are we wit

nessing in
this sun-a

massing snow–
receptive

day a pre
view to summ

ertime's ex
pansive

light-call
ings.

If the sea (3)

a) sons mirror

our life-long

inhabiting
s then I'll

b) choose (if

that remain

s possible)
the late Jan

uary snow-re
flecting

c) brightness

of this time–

intruding wint
er's awaken

ing.

He's back

again that
strangely a

cending bee
tle figureat

ively ans
wering my win

dow's snow–
timed calling

s.

And yet

these leaf–
bared bran

ches still
attuned to

the cold wint
erly wind'

s unsettl
ing reflect

ive–exposure
s.

Are these (3)

a) wintered

birds simply

unable to
climb the moun

b) tainous south

ward's-reach

Are they a
fraid or home-

tending as

c) the biblical

Jacob to where
they sense a

lasting-belong
ingness.

It seem (3)

a) s much easier

to hold two

small nation
s together

b) (however se

parately in

tended) as
Tito's Yugo

slavia than

c) an immense

ly divisive–
América since

its early
founding-day

s.

Faux pas (3)

a) For those

who think

and talk so
quickly unin

tentional

b) ly letting

their safe
guards down

faux pas'
of this or

that sort

c) become an

habitually–
repetitive

most–disturb
ing occurren

se.

For an habit (2)

a) *ual writer*

the moment'

s the ideal
time for grasp

ing that unattend

b) *ed word-sense*

to its most–
fulfilling

and contempla
tive need

s.

With her hus (7)

a) band's alcohol

ic tendencie

s She took to
the grand-tour

b) Evangelical

s first but

in time too
self-enclosing

culturally–
foreigned

c) then the only

Roman Catholic

church I know
with a full

daily program

d) spiritual in

tellectual
cultural but

for the most
personal pri

vate needs

e) she found a

mini lakeside
order which in

time didn't

f) personally work-

out so she re
turned home

to her aging
mother and an

eucumenical

g) one Sunday

here the
next there

now fully re
ligiously-

routed.

Corona-timed *(4)*

a) Rosemarie

first those

Bavarian
most-chosen

pretzen coff
ee-timed Poet

b) ry 2nd after

perhaps an outside

ping–pong inter
lude all part

of a daily
Corona most

intimately

c) perfectly-

sourced
schedule with

evening read
ings mostly

now of Chinese
and Spanish

d) poetry and the

finest of news

papers to keep
me/us daily

fit "early to
bed early to

rise"…

If Biden *(3)*

a) manages to

bring togeth

er main-stream
Democrats and

b) non-Trumpian

Republican

s he may act
ually be

c) able even at

78 to help

heal America'
s so divisive-

wound
s.

If you treat (2)

> *a) the dead with*
>
> a real–rever
>
> ence you'll
> think and feel
>
> of them not
> angelical

> *b) ly wingèd but*
>
> with a down-
>
> to-earth real
> ism as alive
>
> now as they
> once and should
>
> always–remain.

Thaw (3)

a) weather as

today's in

the lower-50
s melting a

b) way some of

what's hard

est taken-
hold of my

oft ever-re
acting fear

c) ful though

for my age

still robust-
constitut

ion.

On the way (4)

a) *back home*

from Illmen

see to Otto
brunn a pict

b) *ture-book view*

of the entire

range of not-
so–distanc

ing mountain

c) *s somehow*

claiming not
only a fully–

sensed aesthe
tic–response

but also of

d) *awe for our*

Creator's
unlimited

poetic–re
source

s.

This oncom *(3)*

a) ing winter

night's draw

ing time clo
ser to its

b) essential

ly January

cold-uphold
ing appearan

ces and the
activating

c) warmth of

our almost

60 year's
timely-to

gether
ness.

Sunrise (2)

a) on this cold

winter morn

ing as if
the sky's

been lifted
from its im

b) pending dark

ness to the

inspoken blue
of an ines

capable classi
cal-clarity.

As a Jew (4)

a) *particular*

ly here in

Germany I've
become while

b) *still remain*

ing especial

ly ever–sen
sitive to what

seems to me

c) *a distancing*

from my very
being a neigh

bor though
seldom seen

d) *passing me*

by as quickly

as her lithe
feet could

possibly re
spond.

Time-sharing *(3)*

> *a) We've rarely*
>
> shared a comm
>
> on sleep-rou
> tine I'm an

> *b) early goer*
>
> Rosemarie'
>
> s a late
> responder
>
> So we center
> our other

> *c) wise rhythm*
>
> ic-being to
>
> the mid-day
> of an appre
>
> ciable time-
> sharing.

A Fairy-Tale (3)

a) Land Driving

through the

Schwarzwald
in mid-winter

b) the woods pre

senting their

finest snow–
clothed appear

ances as if
we too had be

c) come a part

of what Heine

called "Ger
many a winter

fairy-tale
land".

As Rosemarie (3)

a) s father once

experienced

some skiers
became for a

b) short-time

blinded from

the bright
ness of the

January sun–
reflecting snow

c) similar to

what Saul later

St. Paul exper
ienced on the

way to Damas
cus.

A Different (2)

a) People The East

Germans after

two dictator
ships have be

come histori
cally other

b) wise formed as

many East Euro

pean states
under the long–

time tenure of
The former

Soviet Union.

Flag-Wavers (4)

a) We as a fam

ily were never

flag-wavers
nor did we

b) find a "pledge

allegiance

to the flag"
in good taste

While the nation
al hymn remain

c) s both poetical

ly and musically

in need of a
great Haydn or

even a once-
considered

d) Dvorak to do

it most suit

ably if even
patriotical

ly so.

Is taste a (7)

a) *question of*

upbringing –

I remained
through my

b) *childhood*

tutered by

the hit par
ade and popu

lar musical

c) *s Or is it*

a question
of personal

make-up –
Until my Bar

d) *Mitzvah I re*

mained a
sports-talker

loud-mouthed
and of in

e) sufficient

quality Who

and what was
it Perhaps my

Bohemian sis

f) ter Lois'

"If you have
n't read Dostoy

efsky you haven'

g) t lived" After

that slowly but
surely my taste

began to find–
itself-out.

Perspective (4)

a) s Are these

various win

ter birds
more fearful

b) of those al

most insurmount

able highlight
s than the mi

gratory one
s or are they

c) more courag

eous by will

ing to take–
on the long

winter cold
ice and snow

d) It depends

on your per

spective
but most es

pecially on
their

s.

He maintain *(4)*

a) ed that Merkel

(a scientist

by training)
showed sign

s-of-stress
of a too-long

b) reign of some

16 years Not

only her new
ly tired-express

ion – we've
no T. V. to

check-up

c) on that But in

her unscienti
fic newly ex

pressive emot
ionalism –

Is that really
a sign of weak

d) ness or of a

continually

engagement
for the welfare

under Corona of
her German peo

ple.

Talk-show *(4)*

a) s have become

a mini-form

of Germany
democracy

b) willing to

argue a point

from each and
every possi

ble angle

c) let the more

so-called ex
perts become

self-express
ive the more

d) one realise

s their lack

of unifying
answers – yes

democracy-
in-action.

A post Trump (3)

a) ian "America

first" or an

Israeli extra
money to be

b) come as a

nation vaccin

ated first
While Germany

now on its

c) moralising

post-war
high-horses

left-out-in
the-cold.

Though (4)

a) *Trump turned*

out (or better

put) always
remained a

b) *liar and cheat*

Two abilitie

s of his I
continue to

admire His

c) *standing-up*

against tradit
ional views as

on abortion
and Israel

d) *and his (good*

or bad) mostly

doing (if he
could) what

he promised
to do.

Cloud-worship (4)

a) *per If I'd*

been of a primi

tive primieval
nature instead

b) *of worshipping*

sun moon and

stars I'd chose
the clouds in

stead so eas

c) *ily limiting*

the sun's power
ful-scope while

presenting a
heavenly panor

d) *ama of ever-*

changeable

aesthetic-
expressive

ness.

Unreliable (2)

a) If you're de

pendent on

him and he
proves to

be unrelia
ble then lis

b) ten careful

ly to what

he has to
say but then

only with
one ear.

Good grade *(2)*

a) s remain no

guarantee

for success
in the future

Theory and

b) practice often

don't satisfy
a together

ness of under
standing–

purposed.

Half-deaf (2)

a) *Those half-*

deaf as I'

ve become
in time

most only
realising

b) *shadows of*

a once–upon–

a–time world
now eluding

a sense of
self–certain

ty.

Transition (4)

a) al In these

Corona time

s those im
prisoned in

b) semi-loneli

ness no long

er allowed
most person

al contact

c) and amusement

come to real
ise that a-

world-without
may have be

d) come transit

ional to a-

world-that-
isn't any

more.

The Yellow *(5)*

a) Cross Gauguin

may have look

ed-down upon
the faith of

these Breton
ese women

b) while he

painted them

in prayer-ac
cord with their

very raison

c) d'être The

crucified
Christ not

only part of
a personal

d) testament

while height

ened as Creat
or of the

e) landscaping-

background

Convincing
religious art

by a non-be
liever?

A generat *(7)*

a) ion of artist

s and intell

ectuals rais
ing themselv

b) es above the

(for them)

old-fashion
ed and self-

limiting faith

c) while unable

to answer the
perfection

of this (His)
created world

d) Incapable of

realising

the source of
that life-re

newing and

e) daily most-

essential-
love and pa

trons of the
finality of

f) death's self-

realising

claims Never
theless it

g) becomes diffi

cult to feel

pity for such
foolish-arro

gance.

Light-blue (3)

a) curtains These

innocent–appear

ing light–blue
curtains sym

b) bolising a

sense of per

sonal intima
cy while o

pening or
just closing

c) a windowed-

world outside

or even in
side an in

dwelling–va
cancy.

Appropriate- (4)

a) conclusion

s Now a bit

earlier 7:30
lifting the

b) darkness from

those phantom-
obscuring

steadily self-
realising

houses while
down-the-block

c) they've levell

ed the only

other pre-war
example of

changing time
s and hous

d) ing's so-call

ed time-intend

ing appropri
ate-conclus

ions.

Left-behind (4)

a) ers Those left-

behind in the
exalting name

of progress
Trump voiced

their future
less concern

b) s as American-

firsters often

out-of-work
with little

or no pros
pects for the

future Christ

c) ianing basic

conservative
old-fashion

ed patriotic-
family value

s which at
times spilled–

d) over in to

radical right–

wing even rac
ist ideologie

s Joe B. what'
s the sufficient

bait for them?

Landscaping *(3)*

a) nakedness Win

ters' cold–

time rain
s washing a

b) way the last

remnants of

the snow's
radiating

brightness
while we're

c) just beginn

ing once a
gain to feel

that landscap
ing–naked

ness.

Outused- *(3)*

a) cause Now af

ter these

torrential
rains it's

b) cooled-down

to these in

nocent slight
ly-felt snow

flakes as if

c) time had re

considered
its already

out–used
cause.

Advertising (2)

a) and propaganda

two of the

most–used
means of de

meaning lang
uage's own

b) self-insist

ing need for

a newly–sen
sed cleans

ing–appear
ance.

After read (4)

    a) ing Du

    Fu's descript

    ion of his
    young son's

    dying-hunger

    b) he remained

    unable to pre
    vent even with

    his continu
    ing guilty-feel

    c) ings I became

    quite willing

    to subscribe
    as well to

    his centurie'

d) s long wait

ing for a
genuinely

authorized–
recognition.

Drunken *(5)*

a) ness which for

many poets

(not only Per
sian or Chin

ese) seems to

b) release their

poetic–inhabit
ions Whereas

witnessing
such self–de

meaning be

c) havior I'd pre

fer taking to
my classical

ly word–orient
ed poetic–re

traint The

d) sources of

poetic inspira
tion remain as

widely var
ied as life–

itself only in

e) itiated when

language be
comes freed

to its own
inherent–ex

pressive
ness.

I could perhap (3)

   a) s identify best

   with those

   free-flying
   milkweed

   b) s or the so

   varied bird

   s flying o
   ver the mount

   c) ain's time-

   reach to their

   tree-expand
   ing marriage-

   nest
   s.

Self-recept

ive Can time
and space be

come momentar
ily desked to

reliable poet
ic-instinct

s however
personal

ly self-re
ceptive.

Why do only (11)

a) Democratic

partied presi

dents become
inaugurat

ed with the

b) comforting

help of spec
ially-selected

poets Good so
at least in

the intent

c) But why do

Republican
elected pre

sidents re
main so cultur

ally-limited

d) Why has the

so New-England-

based provin
cial Robert

Frost become

e) so-to-say

our national
poet Isn't

that an in
direct way

f) of implying

that provin

ciality's
a main-stay
of the nation

al tradition

g) Barber and

Ives my pri
vate choice

s for Ameri
ca's leading

h) composer

s which im

plies a taste
both lyrical

i) ly-sourced

and America

yes alas New
England-orien

ted Though our

j) great novalist

s as Melville
Twain Willa

Cather Faulk
ner and Fitz

k) gerald all re

main together

as all–America
all–encompass

ing.

"Be thankful (6)

　a) for what you

have" Not only

the poems all
prettified

　b) lined-up to

take their

turn but more
than a few of

my best friend

　c) s lining-up

for the impend
ing death–call

First Martin
then Ingo then

d) S. L. now Chung

still alive

thank God but
this and that

bone broken after

e) 2 bladder oper

ations totally
incapacitat

ed I've still

f) Rosemarie

the most valua
ble ,,Be thank

ful for what
you have".

As they say (3)

　　a) *"Life goes on"*

but at our

age after hav
ing left so

　　b) *much behind*

and we may be

even now on
an unpaved

street as the

　　c) *one we exper*

ienced in Sic
ily that just

suddenly stopp
ed-right-there.

Being both

an historical
Jew and a

devout Christ
ian creates

often enough
a two-faced

self-divis
ive exposure

which one
which way.

Poetry (4)

a) s not real

ly a quest

ion of feel
ings nor ulti

b) mately one

of ideas and

most certain
ly not one

of command

c) ing the right

social and
political

attitude
s but of a

d) feelinged

and thought

ful word-ex
pressive

ness.

Why (4)

a) their shutter

s have been

closed–down
for weeks now

b) Are they in

habiting an

extended ski-
vacation Must

they move
suddenly as

c) that once favor

ite Bavarian

restaurant
of ours be

cause of tax-
evasion Their

d) shutters clos

ed-down No

one seems to
know or even

to care why.

"No sooner (2)

    a) said than done"

Middle-aged

losing her
looks in need

of finding a

    b) nother self

Not for appear
ance sake mind

you but for a
new self-dis

covery.

Side-street (10)

a) *ed Whenever*

he'd been seen

in that city
of his father'

b) *s fame he kept*

to the mediev

al side-street
s where neither

he nor his fa

c) *ther as Jew*

s could ever
become especial

ly monument

d) *ed Ever since*

that winter
day when he

at age 20
left his parent

al supervision

e) for a new fam

ily and its
womanly-bait

he remained
hot/cold to

f) his extrane

ous past He

then chose a
life so for

eign to his

g) parents (though

quite similar
to his father'

s prodigal
son's ways and

h) means) that

he remained

untouchably
permanent

ly-distanc
ing The non-

i) Rankean-histor

ical "what

could have
been" remain

s as a continu

j) al question

for so many
parents with

their so far–
awayed sibling

s.

Friendship (12)

a) s sailing their

own special

predertimin
ing route

b) s yet in

most all there

remains out–
of–bounds

areas never

c) or rarely out

spoken while
permanently

situated in
their own right

d) For us with

some it's a

lack of a
religious

conviction

e) With other

s it's an
indifferen

ce to Jews
and Israel

f) for others

a cultural

indifferen
ce especial

ly to my so

g) demanding poetry

But most of
our friend

ships not

h) only survive

but thrive in
their multi–

dimension
al depth–find

i) s Most-import

ant in an on

coming and
lasting friend

ship remain

j) s what one

calls (for a
lack of a

real under
standing)

k) "the person

al chemistry"

If one from
the four-sid

l) ed friendship

dies that must

become once
again newly

self-reveal
ing for three.

It's most (7)

   a) especially

   part of the

   "classical"
   Chinese poetic

   b) identity-

   cause the per

   sonal and writ
   ten exchange

   of poems im

   c) plying a

   collective
   personal and

   historical
   tradition

   d) The once Elis

   abeth Press

   poets often
   took to such

   a relation

e) though some

(including
myself)

may have felt part
of a totally

f) otherwise e

ven dead-trad

ition in my
instance the

g) German-Austr

ian Jewish

classical
ly-transpar

ent poetic-
one.

Ode to the (4)

a) Wind The in

visible self–

determining
direction

b) ed-wind re

mains sover

eign of its
birthed-be

ginning and
the potential

c) scope of an

impercepti

ble end Man
should be glad

of such a
sovereign

d) ty which he'

s so often pro

claimed but
remains unable–

to-fulfill.

Spotty (4)

a) Here and there

only snow-

spots left
large and small

b) er after those

re-vitalis

ing-rains
somehow

reminding of

c) those spotted

zoo-animal

s and the
spotty insight

s failing to
reveal an al

d) ternate gram

matical-code to

satisfy Warren
and future crit

ics as well.

Churchless (2)

a) Sundays until

that vaccine

's taken-hold
of the necess

ary safe-guard
s Only the

b) resurrect

ion-bells ring

ing through
my more or

less guilty con
science's appar

ent-absence.

To believe (4)

a) that a Jewless

Germany would

solve most all
of the out

b) standing pro

blems But with

no Jews left
to blame for

one's own pro

c) blems Shovel

them out of
their grave

s until we

d) discover o

ther scape
goats of e

qually attend
ant-qualitie

s.

Why do I (3)

a) feel so espec

ially fit (one

can even main
tain dapper)

b) in my Christ

mas' bath–robe–

spendour
perhaps be

cause I'd be
come too used

c) to wearing my

father's out–

used no–long
er–necess

ary–one
s.

Together (4)

a) ness Do we

miss less

frequently
visited dead

b) friends liv

ing at such a

distance than
one's nearby

c) enough to be

so often

visited If
so then death's

domain may

d) be consider

ed more-inti

mate and close
ly guarant

eed.

They've e (3)

    a) ven closed-

down (because

of Corona'
s heedings) all

    b) that's not

functional

ly necess
ary why then

haven't they
allowed the

    c) beauty-parlour'

s most necess

ary fashion
able top–

offs.

A là Swift (4)

a) Only if man'

s greatest ene

my can one
aspire to save

b) the planet'

s animal-life

with all the
beautifying

trimmings as

c) coloring flo

wers and growth-
designed tree

s But then a
bortion kill

d) ing-off poten

cial evil-doer

s may become
ultimately-

justified.

The remain

      ing snow now
      ever-tight it's

      still holding
      to its ground-

      base melting
      my heart's

      length though
      indecisive

      ly.

Looking through *(3)*

      a) glass Can look

      ing-through-

      this window'
      s glass in mid-

      b) winter shut-off

      the wind's cold

      demanding voice
      now indwelling

c) in those realm

s of exposed

and untouch
ably apparent-

silence
s.

That once ex (3)

a) pendable line

Now that once-

expendable
line's narrow

b) ed-down to

his own less

signifying
person words-

in-mind yet

c) closed-in the

length of win
ter's speech

less time-ap
parent pre

sence.

Qualitie (2)

a) s its own

word-guaran

tee It should
be enabled

to stand-up
to time's e

b) lusively

changeable

taste and e
ven the critic'

s dogmatic
self-certain

ties.

Written from (4)

a) Rosemarie's view

(after Li Po)

After almost
60 years one

b) appreciate

s a poet and

lover but the
bills are all

high piled

c) his kiss

es and hug
s as well

but time pre
cludes too

much of that

d) He does his

part but poem
s and love

desire his al
ways very-be

ing.

Northern (2)

> *a) winter sunset*
>
> s with their
>
> dramatical
> ly involved–
>
> coloring
> s impress me

> *b) poetical*
>
> ly more than
>
> those beer-e
> vident tradit
>
> ional Flori
> dian–one
>
> s.

Du Fu and (7)

> *a) Li Po suppos*
>
> edly two of
>
> China's great
> est poets

b) While having read

a full range of

their poems in
translation they

both seemed

c) descriptive

at times auto

biographical
poets even of

the everyday

d) which was at

times hard
for them

while I didn'
t feel in

e) the slightest

the genuine

mark of great
ness Too late

now to learn

f) to read them

in the origin
al. p. s. their

linguistic

g) subtleties

rarely if e
ver distin

guished those
translation

s.

Answering (3)

a) Warren The

feel of a

Jaffin poem
also language

b) wise whether

poetic or di

dactive reveal
s a similar

ity of voiced-

c) expressive

ness Why then
feel about for

an otherwise
visual-presen

tation.

No I'm not (9)

a) question

ing Beethoven'

s greatness
his original

b) ity and his

influence

on later gen
eration

s But I am

c) question

ing his incon
sistent taste

Better if he'
d never writt

d) en those Beet

hovian conclus

ions to two of
the greatest

e) of all possi

ble symphonie

s the 7th and
the enthusiast

ic 9th Beet

f) hoven's the

most heroic
and with his

role-model
Händel often

g) the most con

vincing of

composer
s Yet he tore-

up the dedicat

h) ion of his E

roica to Napol

ean the great
est of all

possible
(French) her

i) oes who left

his beloved

France blood
ied-down to

near insigni
ficance.

140

Some even (4)

　　a) commonly-used

　　themes as

　　"The Masked
　　Ball" have

　　b) lost their

　　once thematic-

　　original
　　ity through

　　Corona's long-

　　c) time masked-

　　presence While
　　even Strind

　　berg's "The
　　Father" (who

　　d) was it?) no

　　longer remain

　　s concealed
　　through the

　　help of mod
　　ern genetic

　　s.

Whether (2)

a) one likes it

or not love'

s possess
ive Jealousy

's the best
prove of

b) that She al

ways referred

to her statu
esque hus

band as "my
Horst".

A freshly (2)

a) time-hold

ing snow

overcame
the visible

and invis

b) ible world that

it alone spoke
with a voice

of indescri
bable self-cer

tainty.

Is snow then *(2)*

a) actually a

voice of re

membrance
not only sug

gesting what

b) had once occur

ed but imitat
ing its awaken

ed and still
renewing-pre

sence.

Even I (2)

a) though half-
deaf could

hear the
crush of my

footstep

b) s designing
that newly
fallen snow

with its own
sense of self-

purposing.

Believe it (2)

a) or not one
of our nut–

attending
squirrels act

ually changed

b) direction

s in mid–air
perhaps re

turning for
a renewing

after–taste.

Yes some Chin *(4)*

a) ese poet (per

haps from the

Tang epoch) in
dicated that

b) the form of

the words ex

pressed should
imitate the

form of the

c) experience

itself Trans
lations could

hardly satis
fy such a

d) commanding

view of the

very-involved-
nature-of-

good–poetry.

It may create (4)

> *a) its own most*

splendid beauty
I mean this
self-perpetua

> *b) ting snow but*

I must shovel-

out the grati
fying remain

s like the

> *c) surprising*

expectation
while on va

> *d) cation of that*

newly emerging

cascade of
poems but once

home I must
type-them-

all-out.

Perhaps (2)

a) *satisfying'*

s the most

poetically-
sufficient-
word for the

b) *encompass*

ing-realm
s of this

continual
ly newly-fall

en snow.

One sense (2)

a) *s that this*

snow as the

wind itself
has been sour

ced by a–

b) *will-of-its-*

own but one
that we could

in–no–way
possibly

understand.

When one *(3)*

a) reads of the

suffering

of million
s of fellow–

b) Christian

s in so many

countries
One begins to

question the

c) depth and in

tent of one'
s personal

ly–encompass
ing–faith.

This self- *(2)*

a) creating snow'

s now merging

in to the
slowly descend

ing wintered
darkness

b) as if re

claiming its

long abandon
ed but still

expectant
ground–base.

Piled-high (3)

a) This snow'

s once again

piling high
the untold

b) reach of my

mind-feeling

ed-poems but
the more I

shovel them
away the deep

c) er they con

tinue to

search-out
their dialog

uing-express
iveness.

As "we hurt (2)

a) those we love

the most" (Strind

berg) I'm still
busy with all

of that unhurt
ing diminish

b) ing my self-

righteous

pride to but
a lowering

winter's
flame.

This land' (5)

a) s now buried

under an in

creasing
depth of snow

b) Is that but

a reflective

self-display
of my own

guiltied pride

c) no longer able

to realise
the weight of

its hurting
instinct

d) s as Ralf G.

once remark

ed so many
years age

"You poet
s have at

e) least retain

ed that spec

ial gift of
writing–off

whatever may
still be dis

turbing you".

Awakening (2)

a) to such a

self-inhabit
ing snow–

depthed per
haps haunting

b) or even clean

sing its still

most disturb
ing blood–in

itiated
past.

America (6)

    a) "home of the

    free and the

    brave" Free
    ing then from

    b) Europe's war-

    drenched con

    tinuity Brave
    enough for

    a new start

    c) often with

    little more
    than the over-

    used and torn
    clothes inhab

d) iting them

Today these
patriotic
words mock

more an Ameri
ca imprison

e) ed in its

own divisive

ness and cow
ardly unwilling

to accept o
therwise

f) perspect

ives than
their own

party-based
ones.

The impend (3)

a) ing height of

this snow's

become so
self-warrant

b) ed guarantee

ing such an

indetermin
able visage

that impede
s even the

c) very identi

ty of my

word-impend
ing growth-ap

pearance
s.

At the road (3)

a) side I came a

cross a dog

(perhaps e
ven a one-

b) time street

dog as Andreas'

and Annette'
s multi-nation

al 4) lick
ing its wound

c) s I passed

him by as

quickly as
I began to

feel my own.

It's a real (2)

a) *long forgotten*

winter this

time no longer
those January'

s Florida-dren
ched-warmth

b) *Time has re*

gained for us

its own self-
certaining

cyclical
know-how.

Battlefield (4)

a) Yes life's

become more

like a battle
field not only

b) between good

and evil bet

ween The Good
Lord and His

Satanic earth

b) ly-situated

rival but also
deeply within

the rivered
claims of our

d) many-sided

diversely-

attending
identity-

cause.

Inky only (7)

a) *a small black*

cocker spaniel

situated at
such times

b) *in the garage*

literally

bouncing
through that

insurmount

c) *able snow-bliz*

zard of '47
to greet us

dog-like the
day after

d) *Inky who ocas*

sionaly brought

us autograph
ed baseball

s from our
neighbor's

e) collection

Inky the watch

dog who only
attacked high

ly perfumed
ladies as

f) Aunt Frida

needed in the

wake of that
terrorising

attack to
be given-away

g) But who need

s a watch dog

only on the alert
for highly-

perfumed-la
dies also

heavily-furr
ed-ones.

This Bavar (2)

a) ian snow's of

self-perpetua

ting quality
always to be

remembered
from the child

b) hood now grown

in to those

(were they real
ly winter's long-

since-forgott
en–one

s.)

A most necess (3)

   a) ary collective-

effort clear

ing the snow
from that e

   b) ver lengthen

ing drive

way car
ed now only

   c) with those

heavily-weight

ed once-time
recollect

ions.

164

The long- *(3)*

a) dead Michael

Butler "I

can't keep
up with you

David" respond

b) ed for me

"Do you think
I can" even

then the poem
s coming at

such short–

c) time interval

s as these
continual

ly recurr
ing snow–re

vival
s.

Superlatives *(5)*

a) The continu

al Trump–like
use of super

latives while

b) still some

what remind
ing of Mark

Twain though
despite his

c) brilliant

wit more like

upstanding
to his ever–

present narcis

d) stic self-pro

claiming
s And what

if those
Californian

olives labell

e) ed only ra

ther-small
medium-size

or even ra
ther-big.

If white' (3)

a) s really a

ground–base

for the to
getherness

b) of all possi

ble coloring

s then though
partially

color–blind

c) I've been so

informed for
realising

only half–
truth

s.

Every (2)

    a) thing here

    's been so

    fully snowed-
    down that I

    find it diffi

    b) cult even to

    look-up to
    my lost image

    's snow-shad
    owing trans

    formation.

Sounds like (7)

    a) Kafka After

    the war with

    the Jewish
    doctors gone

b) and the camp'

s doctors still

around one
could imagine

such a happen

c) ing as this

but not in the
21st century

But it's true
Plagued with

d) abdominal pain

s they diagnos

ed a paralysed
intestine

Home for week

e) s for one of

these Corona
not–performing

operation

f) s At the same

hospital
once again

weeks later
still pained

g) and weak they

claimed her

problem was
to be found

elsewhere.

Thinking

through this
snow-depthed

night the
dark become

s brighten
ed illumin

ed despite
the moon'

s timeful
vacancy.

If you allow

your inner
most feeling

s to speak
you may be

come surpris
ed by their

self-with
holding re

straint.

Why do we (4)

a) have to conform

to Dr. Johnson'

s so strict
grammatical

rules simply a

b) most personal

means of order
ing his Bohem

ian and disor
dered life–

c) style Each

good poem should

fashion its
own most nec

essary rule
s indeed the

d) great Bard

got along with

out Dr. Johnson's
self-improving

grammati
cal-design

s.

This snow' *(3)*

a) creating

its own rhy

thmic sense
of time-tell

b) ing It's mask

ed in inno

cent purity
while it as

Corona her

c) self command

ing almost
unlimited

realm of
whiteness.

Light-blue (3)

a) *curtains Once*

again these

curtain's
light-blue

b) *expressive*

ness remind
ing of Rose

marie's
chaste-modes

c) *ty opening-*

out to a

world now
totally immen

sed in dark
ness.

Poem (2)

a) seemingly

out of no

wheres ap
peared call

ing the hard
ly reluctant

b) poet to a

dialogue

of intense
ly inter

changeable
fruition

s.

The early *(3)*

a) morning Rose

marie and

the late e
vening poet

b) called to

those shadow

ing Hades'
realm un

speakably
immersed in

c) the still

waters of

sleepful-for
getful

ness.

The poet (3)

a) s room still

well over

half-inhabit
ed by its

b) death-whis

pering birth–

time Never
theless window

ed to the
out–reach of

c) the word's

newly awaken

ed self-re
newing expos

ures.

Book shelve (3)

a) s So many

bookshelve

s rowed to
a past time

b) order no

longer deter

mining my
present day

poetic involv
ings or have

g) they secret

ly now and

then aroused
a reactivat

ing past.

Doctor' *(3)*

a) s sometime'

s life-en

dangering
false diag

b) nosing corr

esponds in

a much less
er-important-

way to a
poem innocent

c) ly called

to the wrong

poet's dialog
uing–initia

tives.

Streetlight (3)

a) s There's still

something my

sterious a
bout street

b) light Sudden

ly turned-on

in a darken
ed street

breathing-in

c) a vacancy of

having once
been active

ly-inhabit
ed.

When he re *(3)*

a) leased the un

known intent

of his power
ful voice

b) it rose e

ven beyond the

hightest range
of his most

transcend
ing thought

c) s as a cag

ed-in bird

freed for
its newly-as

piring ascend
ing-flight.

Trying to (3)

a) reread my new

est poetry

book through
the encompass

ing eyes of

b) this or that

particular
reader actual

ly has become
as well an

alternate

c) means of re

consider
ing my own

self-reali
sing-intuit

ions.

This partial (3)

a) thaw's not

only melting a

way this heav
ily-endorsed

b) once-timed

snow–antici

pations but
also the re

sidue of white

c) ness space-en

compassing
the fullness

of its untold-
dominion

s.

I've often *(3)*

a) enough misjud

ged other

s self–anti
cipating in

b) tention

s perhaps be

cause I've
measured

c) them too close

ly to my

own other
wise instinct

ual–reaction
s.

Freedom to be free *(6)*

a) As we left

that enormous
but empty to-

b) the-bones gym

nasium after

our first anti–
Corona shots

such an equal

c) ly enormous

sense of freed
om but freedom

for what No
couples allowed

d) to visit no

concerts movies

plays Yes freed
om to be freed

as comforting

e) as impeaching

a president
no longer in

office We could
n't even go

f) out to celebr

ate as all the

restaurant
s remain

closed down.

A world of (3)

a) snow's melting

away Even the

attending snow
man's obligued

b) to follow suit

No real differ

ence from the
sand castles

we built as
children near

c) the sea So we

learn young

that our own
world won't

be lasting
forever.

Does over- (7)

    a) doing-it Walt

    Whitmanes

    que as the
    imperialist

    b) s as the late

    romantics

    indicate a
    too highly

    favoured

    c) sense of self-

    superior
    ity and a

    real lack of

    d) feeling for

    the apparent
    ly simple

    daily things of
    life Knowing-

e) when-to-stop

's a gift
few preacher

s can call
their own

That ever–

f) reaching-feel

ing from the
height of the

pulpit look
ing-down on

familiar well–

g) willing parishion

ers those bib
lical insight

keep coming-on
as if fresh

ly-renewed.

Spanish-Span *(4)*

a) iards Our dedi

cated Spanish

teacher Lopez
once remarked

b) "I can see

a real Span
iard from far

away" That may
be true as

c) well or even

inter–related
to the special

Spanish land

d) scaping his

tory and yes
specially

Spanish–form
ed poetry.

Complement (8)

a) ary She

home-bred
and biblical

ly-oriented

b) remained satis

fied with the
fruits of

the land as
apples and

pears Where

c) as he a wander

ing Jew by na
ture loved

those exotic
fruits as

d) mangos and pa

payas That re

mained but one
form of their

complementary
marriage She

e) a blond fully-

formed German

beauty while
he the dark

Judaic-type

f) – Opposite

s attract
they say by

form taste
and inclina

g) tion as long

as a basic

common-ground
as faith re

h) mains as a

guarantee

for their lov
ed–together

ness.

Our prayer- *(3)*

a) list for sick

and perhaps

dying friend
s continue

b) s to grow

as if the

Angel of Death
and his assis

tants had mark

c) ed-them-and-

us off for
that so-called

"special treat
ment".

Yet Yet Yet *(5)*

a) Yes the post-

war Germans
have consist

ently come–

b) to-grips with

their Holo
caust–guilt

but mostly
after the

c) chief offend

ers had died–

off while 2015
letting unmarked

anti-semetic

d) Muslims through

their open
borders and

while consist

e) ently display

ing a lack-of–
support for

Israel in the
United Nation

s.

Tiny but (3)

a) colorful win

ter birds

accentuat
ing the naked

b) ness of these

snow-releas

ing branch
es just mot

ionlessly
proclaim

c) ing their own

self-distin
guishing here

I'm on momen
tary-display

s.

These once (2)

a) accumulat

ing yester

day's snow's
now half-thaw

ing but still

b) weighing hea

vily on
short-lived

but now un
timely-remem

brance
s.

It must re (4)

a) main as a

living stigma

for those
numerous

b) children

(especial

ly here in
Bavaria)

of SS murder
ers Their

c) names as comm

on as Eichmann

Bohrmann and
Goebbels ...

whereas Hein
rich Himmler'

d) s daughter

(quite an ex

ception) re
mained proud

of her al
ways-loving-

father.

Looking away (5)

a) (a problem

matic not only

German tenden
cy most espec

b) ially common

during those

devastating
12 years)

Now having

c) looked away

from the new
elected Ameri

can president'
s foreign

d) policy simil

ar in many re

spects to his
demonised-pre

e) decessor Or

can one also

label it as
wishful-think

ing.

Little bird (3)

a) as these color

ing ones ex

amplying their
abilitie

b) s right be

fore my ex

pectant eye
s seem to pre

fer swinging

c) on expanding

receptive
ly-endowed lithe

winter branch
es.

Memories of *(4)*

    a) a century past

    American

    politics on
    the street

    b) by left and

    right alike

    propelled
    by a weapon

    ed and radical

    c) minority as

    in Weimar-time
    s can easily

    escalate in
    to a civil

    d) war type of

    bloody and self-

    destructive
    insurrection.

Picture (3)

a) *frames differ*

ently shaped

formed and
colored are

b) *like the*

clothes we

daily wear
predetermin

ing the limit

c) *ed extent of*

our own feat
ured time-en

compassing
expressive

ness.

We may *(3)*

a) associate

certain place

s with cer
tain people

s and the

b) times we've

known them
there But if

we don't re
turn as with

Florida this

c) year they may

disappear
in to those

times of our
still forgott

en-past.

Time and *(3)*

a) space may re

main thorough

ly abstract
for physicist

b) s and mathe

matician

s but for a
sensitive

c) poet they

may actually

reside deeply
within our

very-being.

For a young

girl stars
may be seen

as prettify
ing the hea

vens as the
flowering

designs of
her first

self-signify
ing dress.

Otherwise (3)

a) dialogued

Poems may re

claim their
own special

b) needs for

voicing time

ly-concern
s whereas

the poet

c) must become

intuned for
such preval

ent time-
sakes.

Unlined *(2)*

a) poetry pad

as white as

the time-ex
pressive snow

while the
words themsel

b) ves awaiting

their release

from that im
penetrable

morning dark
ness.

Good poetry (2)

a) resolves that

timely wombed

pregnancy
through ex

pectant yes
outsider

b) words demand

ing an account

able presence
of their own

self-inhabit
ing.

Some person' (4)

a) s most genuine

even rarely

overheard
motives self–

b) designing

appearance

continue
s to remain

foreign e
ven estranged

c) from the daily

timely–prepar
ed know-how

as tracks in
snow (their

d) s) lost in

the nearby
wooded–con

fines.

Those momen (5)

    a) tary most per

sonal exper

tiences seem
of such little

    b) significance

especially in

our Corona de
termining time

s and almost
world-wide

    c) Christian

persecution

s Yet the big
picture's al

ways composed

    d) as a cross-

word puzzle
of tiny irre

gular part
s that must

ultimately

e) come to

gether again
formed from a

pre-determin
ing unity.

That snow- *(3)*

a) time fairy-

tale interlude'

s now almost
entirely wash

b) ed away through

these persist

rains while
leaving behind

a lasting-re

c) membrance

of a purify
ing if only

shortly-sensed
landscaping.

My window' *(2)*

a) s view revealing

(or so it

would seem)
a late autumn

al nakedness
housed with

b) otherwise

neighbor

ing window
s a wind-es

caping dia
logued time-

length.

Developmental Phases *(3)*

a) Most boy

s these day
s seem to de

velop through

b) their chosen

means of trans
portion from

rollers to
three and then

two wheeled

c) bicycles to

that almost
religious

ly unveiling
of a first

genuine-car.

Girls became (2)

    a) for us little

boys like a

lasting nuis
ance flighty

images of an

    b) habitual less

er-breed With
maturity ours

as theirs some
how mysterious

ly transform
ing.

Butter finger (4)

a) *s As a once-*

time left field

er I caught
most everything

b) *in sight e*

ven when noth

ing had been
aimed my way

an occasion
al mosquito

c) *But now in my*

aging year

s so much
keeps slipp

ing through
my finger

d) *s not only*

those lyrical

passages just
ly freed for

their own
time-telling.

For G. H. (3)

> *a) Scraggsville*
>
> Maryland seem
>
> s like an un
> likely place
>
> for a good
>
>
> *b) modern poet*
>
> to be scent
> ing-words-
>
> out much the
> same way as
>
> Breughel's
>
>
> *c) hound-dog*
>
> s instinct
> ively levell
>
> ed-down for
> their game-
>
> calling
> s.

Slow-poke (4)

a) *No one would*

ever have

dared calling
him the 10

b) *or 11 year-*

old speedy

Jaffin "best
athlete in the

sophomore
section" a

c) *slow-poke but*

now after his

afternoon'
s snoozing-off

poking him at
sustaining

d) *intervals seem*

s the only

way of rous
ing him for

coffee-time.

This unsea (4)

a) sonably warm

ing winter wea

ther would
softly remind

b) us as the pre

vious down–

settling snow
s that these

uncertain

c) ing winds have

retained their
own seasonal

deviation

d) s from time'

s recurring
instinctual

rhythmic–pat
tern

s.

These tiny

coloring win
ter birds

darting sudden
ly through

their self-
distinguish

ing time-tell
ing appear

ance
s.

This after

noon's blown-
in-clouds imi

tating their
own pre-deter

mined heaven
ly-distanc

ing
s.

As G. H.

correctly in
dicates the

natural image
itself can

often realise
a plurality

of self-sus
taining express

iveness.

Although (3)

a) the Chinese

poets as the

Persians re
main especial
b) ly dependent

on wine They'

re far less
explicit about

sexuality

c) thereby actual

ly heighten

ing its unspo
ken yet enti

cing-fascina
tion.

Those most (4)

a) *meticulous*

about their

use of lang
uage and the

b) *fineness of*

their psychol

ogical and
social instin

cts as Henry

c) *James for ex*

ample general
ly delimit the

lyrically-

d) *poetic and meta*

physical-relig
ious from their

epochal-land
scaping

s.

Is there an (2)

a) intricate re

lation between

some sport
s as skiing

ice-skating

b) and golf with

the spacial
poetry of dia

logical–inti
macie

s.

Mixed-loyalitie (12)

a) s The so-call

ed "Stalingrad

Madonna"
What are Jesus

and Mary doing
here as Jews

b) when their (our)

peoples are be

ing slaughter
ed daily by the

thousands in
not–so–far a

way–Auschwitz

d) But then a

more distant
but yet more

intimate
painter's a

genuine Christ
ian opposed to

e) Hitler And

"the final

solution" Here
in Stalingrad'

f) s the beginning

of the end

of Hitler's
demonic re

gime.

g) p. s.

The German
Protestant

church either
stood behind

h) Hitler or

passively ac

cepted with few
exception

s the murder

i) of their God

with his entire
Jewish entour

age Even the
Stuttgart con

j) fession of

guilt 1947 not

a single word
about the Holo

caust Is that
a holy church

k) A handful

of Jewish-German-
patriots still

remained either
hidden for those

12 years or re
turning from

l) Israel and else

wheres to re

identify them
selves with the

m) great cultural

nation of their

youth and the
new democrat

ic Germany.

If I said (4)

a) or actually

wrote some

thing posit
ive about the

b) former presi

dent our left–

wing democrat
ic friends would

descend on me
claws first

c) While if I

judged him
too harshly

our Trumpian
friend would

devour my re
mains America

d) divided more

dangerous

ly now than
just before

The Civil War.

These ever- *(7)*

a) insisting rain

s have now

finished–
off their job

b) thoroughly

in the best

or worst Ger
man tradition

Not a single

c) touch of those

former snow–
mounds to be

rediscover

d) ed however

far-reaching
my poetic-eye

s could still
determine This

e) very late

January morn

ing's dark
ness now once

again so na

f) kedly-encom

passing that

I feel the
7:30 need

g) to get wash

ed and dress

ed just as
quickly as

possible.

For the (3)

> *a) world's aging*
>
> "most prolif
>
> ic poet" every
> momentary-

> *b) moment count*
>
> s love-wise
>
> as word-wise
> before that
>
> Shakespear

> *c) ean curtain*
>
> ultimately
> descends upon
>
> Rosemarie
> and himself.

For G. H.'

s "haiku"
Yes every sin

gle syllable
counts most

especially
that spacious

expanse as
an entire world

landscaped–
in-snow.

Strangely (3)

a) self-aware

One must have

felt strange
in those totali

b) tarian state

s being watch
ed as Weinberg

by Stalin's se
cret police

no longer

c) curtained of

one's own
life-endanger

ed artisti
cally-dialog

ued-identity.

For G. H.

Haiku at
its best a

way of capti
vating a sing

gle moment
though not

only for its
own-sake.

Here in Cor (4)

a) ona times

fewer babies

more baby
dogs don't

b) talk back or

habitually
cry when in

need They're
thankful for

each and e

c) very caress

ing moment
Through long

walks they're un
leashing some

of your most-

d) pressing-

thoughts
That's why few

er babies more
young dog

s here.

666 *the bibli* (3)

a) cal Satanic-

number I'm not
superstit

ious though I
do feel a bit

b) uneased when

a black cat

crosses my
path on a Fri

day afternoon
I also under

stand why some

c) of New York'

s hotel's noth
ing between

the 12th and
14th floor

I'm not real
ly superstit

ious.

Those Jew- *(5)*

a) houses never

torn-down

in that town
in central

b) Germany They'

ve remained

vacant for de
cades perhap

s in fear

c) of their ghost

s from the
past or in re

verence for
those "so well

d) integrated"
until The Night
of Crystals
with those Jew–

e) store's glass bro
ken-in and their
goods not-so-
secrectly-stol
en.

The highest (4)

a) *seen tree of*

all that lithe

feminine birch
as a famed

Chinese poet
once remarked

b) *for his time-*

telling eye

s "as a 15–
year-old girl

so slender
and graceful

c) *ly formed" But*

why then
do so many

remain in the
coldest North

d) *em least in*

habitable part

s of Canada
still so grace

fully-form
ed.

Symbolical (2)

a) ly revealing

The coloring

fishes in
those Chinese

fish-bowls
somehow glass-

b) revealing

symbolical

ly and aesthet
ically their

imprisoned
no-ways-out.

Baby-faced *(3)*

a) Has he come

to look that

way because
he's really

b) young-at-heart

Something haunt

ing about this
look-of-his

Only later did
I realise he'

c) d been through

the camps and

remained real
ly much older

than he actual
ly appear

ed.

Only 83 *(4)*

> *a) A quick after*
>
> noon nap as
> those Madison
>
> Avenue stand
> ing business–
>
> *b) lunches More*
>
> important
>
> things yet to
> be done My
>
> father remain
>
> *c) ed that way*
>
> until his 90th
> and the life–
>
> summarising

d) fall Not out

of tune with
this love and

poemed life
yet only 83.

Safe in the (5)

a) suburbs not

black or other

wise-colored
carefully se

b) cluded from

life's danger-

zones Any talk
of death and

dying out-of-

c) bounds learned

of the holocaust
quite late and

from outside-
sources Over-

d) protected one

might say That'

s the why and
where fear has

e) staked its

plot so deeply

felt right at-
the-heart-of

him.

Even in voice (5)

a) less dreams

Some people

especially
certain type

b) s of teacher

s and minister

s never stop
speaking per

haps even in
their voice

c) less dream

s whereas I

never stop
writing It

all started in
my childhood

d) with that too-

much-of-speak

ing-thing
But now with

my ever-will

e) ing pens in

hand it's
spreading it

self out e
ven page-wise.

G. H.

If it's re

peatedly
the same voice

you hear as
with birds

of the same
species then

it must be
genuine.

To the memory (4)

a) of Meng Chiao

You lost your

son to those
very tender

b) years I lost

mine much la

ter He left
on his own

accord not

c) as your son

at The Good
Lord's will

We mourn to

d) gether as

poets hard
ly divided

centurie
s apart.

Lip-service (5)

a) For some

their faith

had become
in time only

b) lip-service

imitating the

forms of what
once spoke to

them intimate
ly-personally

c) For others

their marriage

had become
little more

than a daily-

d) routine with

the prescribe
ed–kiss while

leaving for
work But lip–

service has

e) remained for

us the sens
ual route to

our very soul
ed–love.

Both of my *(4)*

a) elder sister

s Lois and

Doris now liv
ing their Cor

b) ona-timed-lone

liness with

little or no
contact to

the outside

c) world while

we're too
distanced

in every sense
of the word

d) to help re

lieve the i

solation of
their once-

together
ness–world.

I continue (4)

    a) to admire Rose

    marie's abil

    ity with those
    important de

    b) tails of every-

    day-life while

    once recount
    ing to my mo

    ther (who took
    over 2 decade

    c) s to fully

    accept her as

    a bona fide
    daughter)

    why she's the
    ideal mate

    d) for me My mo

    ther surpris

    ingly p. s. it
    "and she's

    bright too".

Light-warmth revival (3)

a) Does the win

ter January-

February
cold actual

b) ly overcome

its tenacious

and most per
sonal grasp

while daily
lengthen

c) ing the sun-

span of its

long-to-be–
awaited light–

warmth–reviv
al.

Poet-in-Re *(4)*

a) sidence for

the personal

ly unknown
Stephan Owen

b) Reviving the

long question

ed reputat
ion of the

great Tang
poet Meng

c) Chiao among

the full-range

of your many
scholarly in

sights and
poetically-

d) enduring-trans

lations makes

you almost
one-of-us

a poet-in-re
sidence.

That unusual (3)

a) *ly slim snow-*

through-the-

night perhap
s to be re

b) *ceived as a*

kind of be

lated remem
brance

c) *for the once*

so fully land

scaping snow
ed-down white

ness-purity.

Autobiograph (3)

a) ical All poetry

(whether we real

ise it or not)
remains in

b) one sense or

another auto

biographi
cal because

its very ex
pressive

c) ness speak

s out of the

depth of our
not yet poeti

cal–intuit
ion.

Is this (4)

> *a) continual*
>
> ly alternat
>
> ing snow–rain–
> snow interval

> *b) s more like*
>
> the two-phased
>
> great French–
> Christian pain
>
> ter Georges

> *c) de la Tour*
>
> first sinful
> ly-nakedly
>
> revealing

d) then the birth-

of-Christ's
purifying

light-radian
ce.

It could only (5)

    a) be described

as a sense-

of-loss caus
ed perhaps by

    b) the nakedness

of that washed-

away-snow Was
it the close

friends recent

c) ly lost or a

lack of home

if and when
Rosemarie

should die

d) Perhaps I'm

too easily
landscaped

anew by that
changeabil

e) ity of time

and place

that not so
certain a

wareness
mood-sensed.

If my physio (3)

a) therapist had

his way I'd

become nothing
more than a

b) series of ex

ercises here

for the mus
cles there for

the bones I'm
beginning to

c) feel most like

those skeleton

s inhabiting
his dead–set

room
s.

Matthew (6)

a) my nephew and

favorite of

his generat
ion lost his

b) mother today

though his par

ents never
lost him He

remained in

c) the best sense

of that word
a family-orient

ed Jew though
he never found

d) ed a family

of his own

and knew
little if

nothing of
his Jewish

e) non-faith

We feel deep

ly his loss
and his un

fulfilled
need for a

f) wife children

a family he
could now

call-his-
own.

This day (4)

a) the day of

my eldest sis

ter's death
and her young

b) est son Matt

hew's call re

mind me of
the day our

own son left
house and home

c) for a new be

ginning not

ours but his
that slight

sadness–feel
ing of newly

d) fallen snow

and the immen

se distance
he would

leave behind–
him.

The unsaid- *(3)*

a) said it still

remains the

unsaid that
affects us

b) most-of-all

Words when

newly releas
ed open-out

the vast un

c) spoken space

that-pre-de
termines our

own sense of
very-being.

Prodigal (4)

a) Son for Manfred

Siebald How

much did I
become the

b) Prodigal

Son leaving

safely-secur
ed house and

home for a

c) people not

long ago des
stroying The

Father's home
stead to which

d) I returned

to my real

father's
faithful ever–

timely
ness.

Not only (5)

a) have we stolen

the first–birth

ed rites of
the all-creat

b) ive's God's

self-determin

ing will but
we continual

ly desecrate

c) the beauty of

his creatur
ed fulfilling

ness while a
mong others

d) violently

stealing the

archaic ele
phant's self–dis

e) tinguishing

tusks Money–

minded man
the highest of

his creation
s?

Alchemist (Spitzweg) (3)

a) The alchemist

tries to trans
form base metal

b) s in to gold

and silver
while we al

chemist-poet
s transform

a cliché

c) used-out

language in
to the gen

uine shine
of freshly-

minted coin
s.

Perhaps we've (4)

   a) birthed an Ein

stein or two

but why call
us a special

   b) ly talented

people Where

are our Bach
s and Beethoven

s Michelangelo'
s and Donatello

   c) s Rembrandts

and Giottos

Shakespeare
s and Tolstoi

s ...
We're only spec

   d) ially gifted

by being recept

ively called
to become God'

s chosen-peo
ple.

Lullaby (4)

a) There's

something
serenely self–

inhabiting
about fresh

b) ly fallen

snow It set

s my mind
off to creat

ional contem
plations of

c) Christ's puri

fying satisfact

ions Rosemarie
in soft blue

fashions for
me an untouch

d) able noctur

nal design of

moon stars and
otherwise

nightly child
held-blessing

s.

Was that hea (2)

    a) vily wrinkled

    surface of

    the aging
    passion fruit

    mocking our

    b) feeling so

    youthful-at-
    heart and

    future-orien
    ted time-

    sense.

Falling' (7)

a) s one of those

multi-meaning

English word
s Falling-in-

b) love describe

s the off–

balancing of
one's entire

being Such a

c) falling's a

symptom of
love-sickness

Falling as
leep implie

d) s another

and darkly

levelled
sense-of-be

ing While the

e) fall in such

simple word
s means aut

umn character
ised most signi

f) ficantly

through the

habitual fall
ing-of-leave

s I must
now steady

g) my poetic-

self to count

er the side-
effects of

such falling
ness.

Translation (5)

a) s How can one

judge the qual

ity of poetic
translation

b) s if one does

n't understand

the original
That's only

possible if

c) the translat

ion stands–up
on its own as

good poetry
in its own

d) right But what

if the trans

later's a poet
himself as

e) Ezra Pound'

s Chinese trans

lations – whose
poem will it

become.

No one (4)

a) *should doubt*

the original

ity of Garcia
Lorca's poetry

b) *nor of its in*

trinsic Span

ishness But
as much ear

lier Spanish

c) *paintings*

there's a blood–
strain predeter

mining Lorca's

d) *insistant imag*

ery Is that all
in part a hang

over from the
Reconquista.

Tiredness *(4)*

a) the greatest

hindrance

to my creat
ivity It

b) blunts the

necessary

self-purpos
ing It repres

ses the clar
ity of my

c) self-illumin

ating imagina

tion It's con
tinually call

ing for a
sleepful inter

d) lude while Poem

wide-awake

just waiting
for a continu

ous-dialogu
ing.

It's now (6)

      a) 27 years since

      I left my

      only parish
      Malmsheim

      b) Those under

      40 can hard

      ly remember
      me as "The

      Jewish minist

      c) er" while those

      over 40 can
      hardly forget

      my German Faux
      Pas "The assem

d) bly of used-

clothes on the

coming Monday"
One of my best

confirmants

e) came home after

his first con
frontation in

struction "Mo

f) ther what the

Reverend Jaffin

told us is
serious really

very serious".

Disgrace *(3)*

a) He fell in

to disgrace
a place so

deviously

b) situated

that there
appeared no

clearly mark
ed route for

c) getting him

out of its

haunted for
estal-terr

ain.

Letter-of-the *(2)*

a) Law It became

necessary in

these Corona
times to re

open that
letter-of-the

b) law at least

weekly to

become certain
of its present–

day authentic
city.

Doomsday *(4)*

a) became so e

ver–recurr

ently located
in that sect'

s message of

b) times to come

that it seem
s to have per

manently escap
ed through their

rhetorical back

c) door Unbeliev

able Allan

became so
attached to

that haunt
ing ever-pre

d) sent phrase

that it became

in time un
believably

even daily
self-certain

ed.

February 1 *(4)*

a) Finally made
it through
that first–
time January

b) here at home
in Germany for
at least two
decades It sim
ply lacked

c) that histori
cal even
personal authen
ticity that we
attributed it

d) *(as most every*

thing these day

s) to the back
door's working

of Corona.

One Pleasure *(5)*

a) *It's allow*

ed we heard

it twice (just
to be certain)

b) *on the radio*

One of the

few pleasure
s in these

Corona time

c) s Yes we've

a visitor
this evening

If her husband
Ingo hadn't

d) died a half-

year ago it

would have
been forbidden

Verboten!

e) Nor can she

invite both
of us back

One pleasure
no more!

This *(now) (3)*

a) February

weather has

eased hard
ly a touch

b) of wind just

an immovable

silence per
soning itself

nameless yet
pre-occupied

c) as some per

sons we've

known mainly
Schwabian

Pietist
s.

Yes it's (4)

a) most particu

larly language

as with Shakes
peare's Sonnet

b) s that makes

a poem spec

ial and it
often comes

by itself

c) seemingly un

invited as a
stranger

entering
that often–

d) used door

its word-voice

becoming dia
logically-

present.

One could *(2)*

a) call it a

warm recept

ion like
meeting an

old friend
for the first

b) time in week

s bodying

oneself right
up to that

facial–glad
ness.

How Chinese (4)

a) poet's reputat

ions become

tossed–about
by so–called

b) critical reac

tions most

often caused
(as today right

here and now)

b) by political

and social at
tidudes With

the earlier

d) Chinese it was

a result of
Confucian Budd

hist and Tao
ist concern

s.

Why Haydn of all (5)

a) composers Because

I can always

listen to him
because he make

b) s me inwardly

satisfied – I've

little need of
Beethovian pathos

Because he's al

c) ways innovative

and form–creat
ive Because his

adagios reach
to the very

d) depths Because

his naïve faith

suits me very
well Because

e) of his impecc

able craftsman

ship Because
…!

Yes a relat *(3)*

a) ionship of

three instead

of the usual
four neverthe

less continu

b) ed to sail

its own unim
peded way

with perhaps
otherwise

chosen theme

c) s but with a

continu
ity of a Christ

ian and famil
ied familiar

ity.

A Resumée (5)

a) Bach her

very early
devoted musi

cal personal
ity in time

b) Christian

ed to what'

s commonly-call
ed The 5th

Gospel But

c) form-certain

ed for her
by his danced–

impulses a
theme quite

d) foreign for

Pietist devot

ées his time-
flowing–fluen

cy though

e) quickly agreed

to the at time
s too-much-so

Beethovian
dramatic–

heritage.

Off-timed (4)

a) Some insect

s not necess

arily the
more flutter

b) ing-colored-

ones came out

of their win
ter's sleep

when the mid–
winter weather

c) turned-on a

self-decept

ive warmth
taken-in by

wishful
thinking

d) Such a

spontaneity

actually quite
human at-the-

very-least.

At Face Value (3)

a) *That unfin*

ished even im

perfect feel
ing about a

b) *poem seemed*

to be feeling

much the same
way we eyed

each other

c) *mind you not*

for long and
took that back–

to–work–call
at face–value.

Too late to (4)

a) change course

Once a "real

minister" al
ways so to

b) that last bib

lical–breath

But he did
change not

chameleon–

c) like but to

a former–call
ing now rees

tablish

d) ing its other

wise call as
migratory

birds return
ing home.

Imprisoned (4)

a) Old-age home

s however qual

ity-wise they'
ve become the

b) first and fore

most victim

s of Corona'
s timely-assess

ments They're

c) imprisoned

in a not-visit
er and no-ways-

out existenc
ial existence

d) much like zoo

ed-animals no

longer able
to roam free

ly self-in
habiting.

Du and Sie *(3)*

a) She half-com

plained that

his usual Du
for closeness

had been mo

b) mentarily

replaced with
a more-distan

cing imperson
al Sie for

somehow im

c) plying a lack

of inner re
lation to his

better-than–
self poetis

ing.

Spelling-it- *(4)*

a) out As spell

ing once a

usual streng
th of his not-

b) so efficient

ly distancing

from the rule
s and regulat

ions of tradit
ional grammar

c) now not alway

s sufficient

ly claimed
as a kind of

safety-valve
while spell

d) ing-out his

inherently

voiced instin
ctual know-

how.

For Solvey *(8)*

a) Is how-to-pre

form Bach a

personal
question of

b) taste romanti

cally-sourced

as with Mendels
sohn and Ramin

or closer to

c) Bach's own in

tentions (what
ever they may

have been Is
it pre-deter

d) mined by a

Baroque dance-

like freeing-
expressive

ness or a need

e) to remain true

to Bach's own
mathematical

sense of self–
restraint

f) Should Richter'

s strong vital

ity be replac
ed by a more

transparent

g) singular

ity Personal
ly I prefer

his more com
pressed John

Passion to

h) the over

long Matthew

with its so
repetitious

de capo a
rias.

Fences *(4)*

a) are put there

(Robert

Frost) to
protect what'

b) s sacred for

each–of–us

I wouldn't
tread on

dear friend'

c) s home-ground

if I hadn't
realised an

underlying

d) consensus

of an at time
s otherwise

emphasizing–
taste.

The taste (6)

a) of serious

creative art

ists may seem
somewhat eccen

b) tric to out

siders because

for some-such-
artists their

(if possibly)

c) changing taste

may become in
tricatedly re

lated to their
innermost

d) artistic de

velopment On

the other hand
the taste of

artists whose

e) writings impress

me as Bourges
love of Walt

Whitman and

f) Browning sim

ply estrange
me but not

from his high–
levelled poet

ry.

Doris and *(6)*

a) Lee fighters

for equal

rights for
blacks in

b) those busing-

days Should

they send
their bright

son Matthew

c) to the better

not really in
tegrated

school of high
er-quality

d) or that school

with its black–

based location
They chose a

gainst their

e) so avid con

victions the
better–quality–

school for
their son's fu

f) ture way via

Harvard Stan

ford and Ox
ford P. S. I

would have
done the same.

They went so (2)

a) overboard

with their

generosity
that we immed

iately called

b) for our spec

ialised driver

s to search
for their o

cean–depth
ed treas

ures.

These repeti *(2)*

a) tive tiny

birds sport

ing such dar
ingly refin

ed–color
s that per

b) haps intensi

ties their fly

ing–free wind–
expressive

sporting–man
oeuvre

s.

Her softly

pillowed
cheeks plea

surably sleep
ing the tropi

cal winds
night–calming

waved express
ive–satisfact

ions.

How easily (3)

a) *Muslims in*

need of a

personal lov
ing forgiv

b) *ing God turn*

to Jesus but

then feeling
that void of

a daily suppor
tive-faith re

c) *turn to their*

full-timed

family-orient
ed inherit

ed-tradition.

Was it a com *(2)*

a) bined effort

Michael Haydn'

s 1771 Requiem
for his dead

daughter

b) and Mozart'

s Requiem
some 20 year

s later for his
own impending–

death.

They'd all be (2)

   a) come fighter

   s each

   with its own
   ways and mean

   s until no
   one dared enter

   b) that ring fear

   ed of being

   knocked-out
   in the first

   or rarely 2nd
   round.

Early Februa *(3)*

a) ry the usual

time of our

return from
Florida but

b) this Corona-

year other

wise–perspect
ived a con

tinuity of

c) time's gradual

ly outspread
ing its once

concealing
brightness.

"It takes (3)

> *a) two to tango"*
>
> Is that a
>
> genuine dia
> logue Einstein-
>
> like between

> *b) time and our*
>
> self or does
> time repetit
>
> ively undis
> turbed path
>
> own future-de

> *c) signs while*
>
> we constant
> ly untimed
>
> by our spon
> taneous life-
>
> style.

Owl-eyed

through
those wood

ed darkness
es as a judge

penetrating
its distanc

ing time-dis
closure

s.

"Les Jeux sont (4)

    a) fait" A locked-

    in lonely soc

    iety Corona
    holds the key

    b) to all those

    old-age-home

    and the
    pleasuring

    places we
    once used

    c) for our own

    timely-satis

    faction
    s She's lock

    ed-us-all-
    in and won'

    d) t let-us-

    out until

    her time'
    s finally

    fully-expos
    ed.

A genuine (3)

a) feel-for-poet

ry remains

an expecial
gift almost

b) as rare as

the so-call

ed poets them
selves Those

who possess

c) it realise

the oft con
cealed-depth

of their own
self-imagin

ings.

Mapped-out *(5)*

a) Some friend

ships almost

demand a new
ly mapped–

b) out sense of

our own ship'

s once so
easily routed

direction

c) It's truly fas

cinating to
follow the

history of
mapped–out

places most

d) especially

our own and
the new dis

coveries
that not only

map–out anew

e) but pre-deter

mine the new
ly sourced

direction
as well.

In Nomine

Domini
February 3, 2021

P. S. (3)

a) *It was one*

of those lean

late winter
's days Those

b) *thin branches*

possessing

neither leaves
snow or pearl-

discovering
rain-drops

c) *to shield*

them even

from Febru
ary's warmly-

felt inter
ludes.

I guess The (3)

    a) Good Lord that

master poet

chose such
brighten

    b) ing colors

for those left–

over winter
birds to cheer–

up the solemn
ity of those

    c) dead-down

late winter'

s so evid
ent–mourn

ings.

Unoccupied *(3)*

a) snow shovel

s in these

dried-out
times remind

b) me of that

quiet kind of

husband
always will

c) ing and ready

to help-out

most especial
ly in times-

of-need.

Poetry books by David Jaffin

1. **Conformed to Stone,** Abelard-Schuman, New York 1968, London 1970.

2. **Emptied Spaces,** with an illustration by Jacques Lipschitz, Abelard-Schuman, London 1972.

3. **In the Glass of Winter,** Abelard-Schuman, London 1975, with an illustration by Mordechai Ardon.

4. **As One,** The Elizabeth Press, New Rochelle, N. Y. 1975.

5. **The Half of a Circle,** The Elizabeth Press, New Rochelle, N. Y. 1977.

6. **Space of,** The Elizabeth Press, New Rochelle, N. Y. 1978.

7. **Preceptions,** The Elizabeth Press, New Rochelle, N. Y. 1979.

8. **For the Finger's Want of Sound,** Shearsman Plymouth, England 1982.

9. **The Density for Color,** Shearsman Plymouth, England 1982.

10. **Selected Poems** with an illustration by Mordechai Ardon, English/Hebrew, Massada Publishers, Givatyim, Israel 1982.

11. **The Telling of Time,** Shearsman Books, Kentisbeare, England 2000 and Johannis, Lahr, Germany.

12. **That Sense for Meaning,** Shearsman Books, Kentisbeare, England 2001 and Johannis, Lahr, Germany.

13. **Into the timeless Deep,** Shearsman Books, Kentisbeare, England 2003 and Johannis, Lahr, Germany.

14. **A Birth in Seeing,** Shearsman Books, Exeter, England 2003 and Johannis, Lahr, Germany.

15. **Through Lost Silences,** Shearsman Books, Exeter, England 2003 and Johannis, Lahr, Germany.

16. **A voiced Awakening,** Shearsman Books, Exter, England 2004 and Johannis, Lahr, Germany.

17. **These Time-Shifting Thoughts**, Shearsman Books, Exeter, England 2005 and Johannis, Lahr, Germany.

18. **Intimacies of Sound,** Shearsman Books, Exeter, England 2005 and Johannis, Lahr, Germany.

19. **Dream Flow** with an illustration by Charles Seliger, Shearsman Books, Exeter, England 2006 and Johannis, Lahr, Germany.

20. **Sunstreams** with an illustration by Charles Seliger, Shearsman Books, Exeter, England 2007 and Johannis, Lahr, Germany.

21. **Thought Colors,** with an illustration by Charles Seliger, Shearsman Books, Exeter, England 2008 and Johannis, Lahr, Germany.

22. **Eye-Sensing,** Ahadada, Tokyo, Japan and Toronto, Canada 2008.

23. **Wind-phrasings,** with an illustration by Charles Seliger, Shearsman Books, Exeter, England 2009 and Johannis, Lahr, Germany.

24. **Time shadows,** with an illustration by Charles Seliger, Shearsman Books, Exeter, England 2009 and Johannis, Lahr, Germany.

25. **A World mapped-out,** with an illustration by Charles Seliger, Shearsman Books, Exeter, England 2010.

26. **Light Paths,** with an illustration by Charles Seliger, Shearsman Books, Exeter, England 2011 and Edition Wortschatz, Schwarzenfeld, Germany.

27. **Always Now,** with an illustration by Charles Seliger, Shearsman Books, Bristol, England 2012 and Edition Wortschatz, Schwarzenfeld, Germany.

28. **Labyrinthed,** with an illustration by Charles Seliger, Shearsman Books, Bristol, England 2012 and Edition Wortschatz, Schwarzenfeld, Germany.

29. **The Other Side of Self,** with an illustration by Charles Seliger, Shearsman Books, Bristol, England 2012 and Edition Wortschatz, Schwarzenfeld, Germany.

30. **Light Sources,** with an illustration by Charles Seliger, Shearsman Books, Bristol, England 2013 and Edition Wortschatz, Schwarzenfeld, Germany.

31. **Landing Rights,** with an illustration by Charles Seliger, Shearsman Books, Bristol, England 2014 and Edition Wortschatz, Schwarzenfeld, Germany.

32. **Listening to Silence,** with an illustration by Charles Seliger, Shearsman Books, Bristol, England 2014 and Edition Wortschatz, Schwarzenfeld, Germany.

33. **Taking Leave,** with an illustration by Mei Fêng, Shearsman Books, Bristol, England 2014 and Edition Wortschatz, Schwarzenfeld, Germany.

34. **Jewel Sensed,** with an illustration by Paul Klee, Shearsman Books, Bristol, England 2015 and Edition Wortschatz, Schwarzenfeld, Germany.

35. **Shadowing Images**, with an illustration by Pieter de Hooch, Shearsman Books, Bristol, England 2015 and Edition Wortschatz, Schwarzenfeld.

36. **Untouched Silences**, with an illustration by Paul Seehaus, Shearsman Books, Bristol, England 2016 and Edition Wortschatz, Schwarzenfeld.

37. **Soundlesss Impressions**, with an illustration by Qi Baishi, Shearsman Books, Bristol, England 2016 and Edition Wortschatz, Schwarzenfeld.

38. **Moon Flowers**, with a photograph by Hannelore Bäumler, Shearsman Books, Bristol, England 2017 and Edition Wortschatz, Schwarzenfeld.

39. **The Healing of a Broken World**, with a photograph by Hannelore Bäumler, Shearsman Books, Bristol, England 2018 and Edition Wortschatz, Cuxhaven.

40. **Opus 40**, with a photograph by Hannelore Bäumler, Shearsman Books, Bristol, England 2018 and Edition Wortschatz, Cuxhaven.

41. **Identity Cause**, with a photograph by Hannelore Bäumler, Shearsman Books, Bristol, England 2018 and Edition Wortschatz, Cuxhaven.

42. **Kaleidoscope**, with a photograph by Hannelore Bäumler, Shearsman Books, Bristol, England 2019 and Edition Wortschatz, Cuxhaven.

43. **Snow-touched Imaginings**, with a photograph by Hannelore Bäumler, Shearsman Books, Bristol, England 2019 and Edition Wortschatz, Cuxhaven.

44. **Two-timed**, with a photograph by Hannelore Bäumler, Shearsman Books, Bristol, England 2020 and Edition Wortschatz, Cuxhaven.

45. **Corona Poems**, with a photograph by Hannelore Bäumler, Shearsman Books, Bristol, England 2020 and Edition Wortschatz, Cuxhaven.

46. **Spring Shadowings**, with a photograph by Hannelore Bäumler, Shearsman Books, Bristol, England 2021 and Edition Wortschatz, Cuxhaven.

47. **October: Cyprus Poems**, with an illustration by Odilon Redon, Shearsman Books, Bristol, England 2021 and Edition Wortschatz, Cuxhaven.

Book on David Jaffin's poetry: Warren Fulton, **Poemed on a beach,** Ahadada, Tokyo, Japan and Toronto, Canada 2010.